Birding hotspots in Andalusia

Huelva province

Gonçalo Elias

Birding hotspots in Andalusia

Huelva province

Title:	Birding hotspots in Andalusia Huelva province
Author:	Gonçalo Elias
Cover page:	Penduline Tit *Remiz pendulinus* (Pedro Marques)
Digital illustrations:	C. Maria Elias
Production:	C. Maria Elias
Printing:	Kindle Direct Publishing
Distribution:	Amazon.com

1st edition, December 2019

ISBN: 978-1081510398

Print On Demand

Contact: goncalo.elias@gmail.com

CONTENTS

Huelva

Lying at the western tip of Andalusia, the province of Huelva covers the area between Seville and the Portuguese border (see map below).

This province is bordered to the north by the Extremadura region (province of Badajoz), to the west by Portugal, to the east by Seville province and to the south by the Atlantic Ocean.

Map of Spain showing the location of Huelva province (shaded in dark grey), Huelva town, and several large cities.

The province covers an area of 10,128 km². Its population is about 520,000 inhabitants (as of 2014); 30% of them live in the capital.

There are 81 municipalities, grouped in six 'comarcas' (see map below).

Map of the six comarcas of the Huelva province

The **Costa Occidental** is mostly a lowland area. The beaches cover the entire coastline and so this region attracts many tourists, especially in summer. Agriculture is also important; there are many greenhouses, the majority of which are used to grow berries. There are several wetlands, mostly small estuaries, as well as pinewoods.

The **Comarca Metropolitana de Huelva** comprises Huelva capital and several surrounding towns, including Gibraleón, Moguer, Palos de la Frontera, and Punta Umbria. It is densely populated, and there are several industrial areas, especially south of Huelva. The Odiel estuary, one of the most extensive wetlands in the province, lies just in the middle of this comarca.

El Condado is a large comarca. It is a flat area, mainly agricultural land, but there are also pine plantations. A big portion of the Doñana National Park, the most important wetland of Andalusia, lies within the Condado.

El Andévalo lies inland, along the border with Portugal. Its landscape is slightly hilly, as it forms a transition area between the coastal plains and the northern hills. Agriculture is intensive, especially in the southern half, and large citrus orchards can be seen along some of the main roads. Woodland consists mostly of Holm Oaks and Eucalyptus, but many hillsides are covered mainly with scrub. There are also a few mines, most of them abandoned.

Cuenca Minera is a mining region. Its landscape is somewhat similar to that of the Andévalo, but with much less agriculture. It comprises a sizeable mine at Minas de Riotinto. The river Tinto flows south towards Huelva. Its waters are extremely acidic and have an intense red colour.

The **Sierra de Huelva** is the largest comarca. It is a mountainous region, rising up to 1050 metres. There are many forested areas, including Cork, Holm, and Pyrenean Oaks, as well as riverine woodlands. Population density is quite low here. Aracena is the most important town; most other towns in the region are rather small.

Birding in Huelva province

The province of Huelva is home to one of the most important wetlands in Spain: Doñana National Park. This vast wetland, which extends eastwards into the neighbouring province of Seville, holds enormous populations of waterbirds, including ducks, geese, waders, terns, herons, and flamingos. There are also many raptors and passerines. It is no surprise that this place attracts countless visitors from abroad, who wish to enjoy the wonders of the southern European birdlife.

However, for the visiting birdwatcher, this province has much more to offer. The Marismas del Odiel, a large estuary in front of Huelva, holds one of the largest colonies of flamingos in Spain and also attracts an array of waterbirds, especially waders and gulls. Along the coast, there are several other estuaries and lagoons, and although they lack the huge numbers of birds present at Doñana, they often hold exciting species, such as Ferruginous Duck, Audouin's and Slender-billed Gulls and Caspian Tern, often allowing close approaches.

Away from the coast, there are also some interesting hotspots. The Campiña de Huelva is a strip of open country, which is a great place to look for birds of prey, including Montagu's Harrier in spring and Red Kite in winter. There are also some smaller steppe birds, such as Calandra Lark. With luck, one may even find the scarce Olivaceous Warbler, which reaches its western limit here.

Further north, around Tharsis and Puebla de Guzmán, there are some old mines, which are home to the elusive Eagle-owl, along with Blue Rock Thrush and the rare White-rumped Swift. In this region one can also see large soaring birds, including Black Stork and vultures.

Finally, in the northern third of the province, there are the hills of Sierra de Huelva. This area holds a large population of Cinereous Vulture, and also many interesting passerines, such as Cirl and Rock Buntings, Iberian Chiffchaff, and Rock Sparrow.

This is the first volume in the series 'Birding hotspots in Andalusia'. In this volume, which covers the westernmost portion of the region, we present a selection of hotspots in the Huelva province, aiming at helping anyone with an interest in birds to get the best birding opportunities.

Hotspots have been selected taking into account bird variety and ease of access. A short description is provided for each hotspot, along with a list of the most interesting birds that can be found there and some suggestions on how it can be explored. GPS coordinates are provided for several reference points. Some species that are common throughout the region, such as House Martin, Goldfinch, or Blackbird, have been left out.

The selection comprises seventeen hotspots. Their distribution by comarcas is as follows:

➤ Costa Occidental

- Isla Canela marshes and beach
- Isla Cristina saltpans
- El Prado lagoon
- Cartaya pinewood
- River Piedras marshes

➤ Comarca Metropolitana de Huelva

- El Portil lagoon
- Odiel marshes and estuary
- Estero de Domingo Rubio
- Palos lagoon

➤ El Condado

- Doñana – El Rocío
- Doñana – La Rocina
- Doñana – Palacio del Acebrón
- Doñana – El Acebuche
- Campiña de Huelva

➤ El Andévalo

- Puebla de Guzmán
- Tharsis

➤ Sierra de Huelva

- Sierra de Aracena y Picos de Aroche

No hotspots have been selected for Cuenca Minera.

The map on the following page shows the location of the various hotspots.

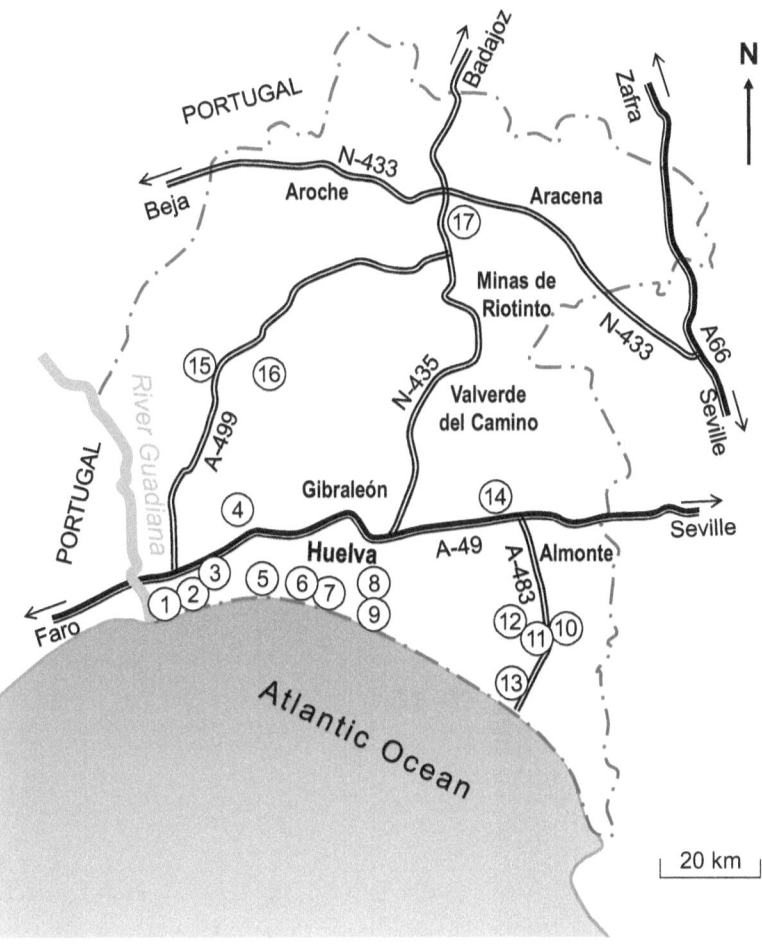

1. Isla Canela marshes
2. Isla Cristina saltpans
3. El Prado lagoon
4. Cartaya pinewood
5. River Piedras marshes
6. El Portil lagoon
7. Odiel marshes and estuary
8. Estero de Domingo Rubio
9. Palos lagoon
10. Doñana – El Rocío
11. Doñana – La Rocina
12. Doñana – Palacio del Acebrón
13. Doñana – El Acebuche
14. Campiña de Huelva
15. Puebla de Guzmán
16. Tharsis
17. Sierra de Aracena y Picos de Aroche

Map of birding hotspots in the Huelva province

Isla Canela marshes and beach

Saltmarsh, old saltpans, and beach.

Birds

Resident: Shelduck, Gadwall, Cattle Egret, Little Egret, Marsh Harrier, Kentish Plover, Yellow-legged Gull, Hoopoe, Crested Lark, Stonechat, Zitting Cisticola, Sardinian Warbler, Spotless Starling, Corn Bunting

Breeding visitors: Montagu's Harrier, Little Tern, Pallid Swift, Red-rumped Swallow, Iberian Yellow Wagtail

Non-breeding visitors: Gannet, Cormorant, Spoonbill, Flamingo, Osprey, Oystercatcher, Grey Plover, Ringed Plover, Knot, Sanderling, Dunlin, Bar-tailed Godwit, Whimbrel, Curlew, Greenshank, Common Sandpiper, Turnstone, Great Skua, Mediterranean Gull, Slender-billed Gull, Audouin's Gull, Caspian Tern, Common Tern, Sandwich Tern, Black Tern, Kingfisher, Crag Martin, Meadow Pipit, Dartford Warbler

How to visit it

Isla Canela lies about 4 km southeast of Ayamonte, close to the Portuguese border, and access is made through this town. There are two areas of interest here: the saltmarsh and the beach. To visit the saltmarsh, follow signs to Punta del Moral. Just before arriving at that location, there is a track to the left signposted 'Sendero Salinas del Duque'. This track leads to a gate (37.1908, -7.3462)

Visits are made on foot only. A marked trail goes around the saltmarsh and is about 5 km long. There are also some old saltpans. The trail goes along a dyke, which separates the saltmarsh and the shore of the river Carreras. Along this route it is possible to see many waders, along with other waterbirds. At high tide, most birds tend to rest in the saltpans, while at low tide they usually feed in the estuarine muds. During the breeding season, the number of birds is much smaller, but Little Terns and usually around and Pallid Swifts often come to feed here.

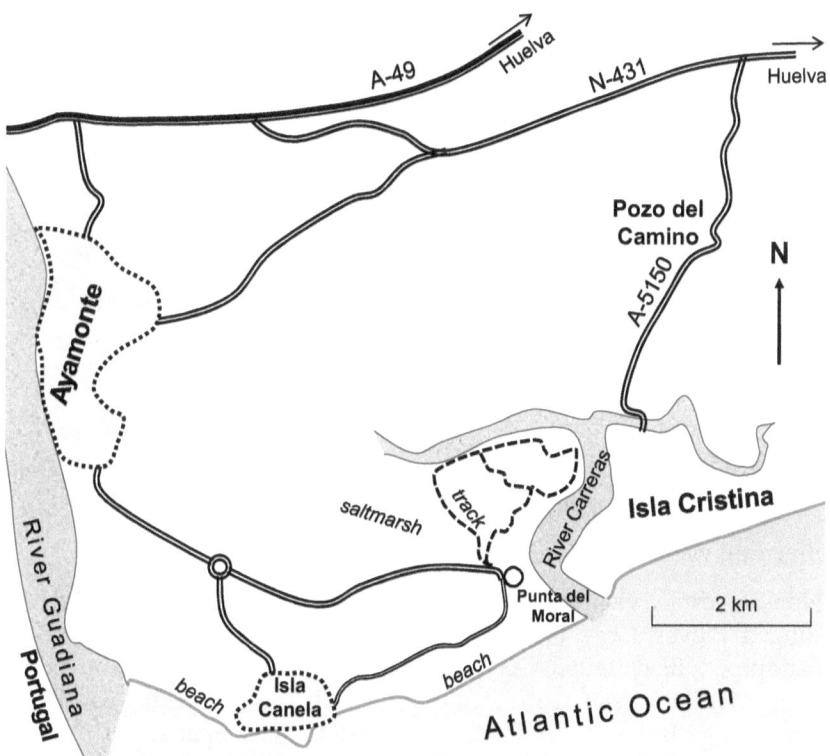

The beach is also worth a look. It is very long (about 6 km) and can be explored in either direction. A good option is to walk westwards until one reaches the Guadiana river mouth. During low tide, there are often sandbanks, which attract large flocks of gulls (including Audouin's and Slender-billed), terns, along with Cormorant, Knot, Oystercatcher and other waders. A look at sea may produce some seabirds, especially when weather conditions are adverse and wind blows from the south.

Isla Cristina saltpans

A complex of saltpans, surrounded by salt marsh.

Birds

Resident: Shelduck, Little Egret, White Stork, Black-winged Stilt, Avocet, Kentish Plover, Yellow-legged Gull, Crested Lark

Breeding visitors: Little Tern, Pallid Swift

Non-breeding visitors: Cormorant, Spoonbill, Flamingo, Osprey, Ringed Plover, Grey Plover, Little Stint, Sanderling, Dunlin, Curlew Sandpiper, Black-tailed Godwit, Redshank, Turnstone, Slender-billed Gull, Mediterranean Gull, Audouin's Gull, Caspian Tern, Sandwich Tern, Crag Martin, Water Pipit, Bluethroat, Spanish Sparrow

How to visit it

Leave the A-49 on the exit no. 122 and follow the signs to Isla Cristina. After passing Pozo del Camino, the town of Isla Cristina is visible just ahead. The best and most accessible tanks (called Salinas de Vistahermosa) are located just north of Isla Cristina. Access is via a dirt road to the right just before entering this town (37.2081, -7.3264).

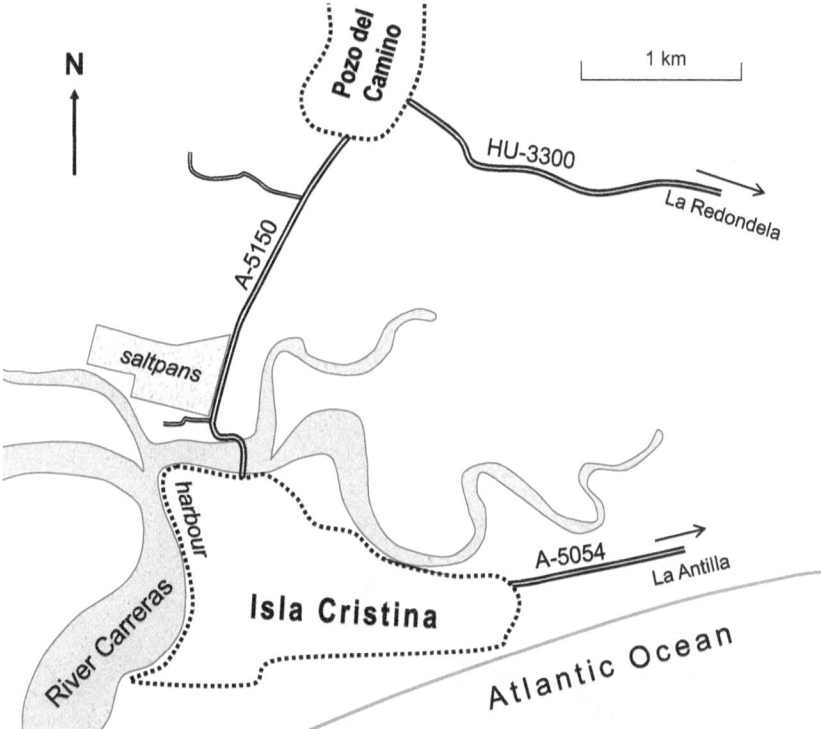

There is a gate preventing vehicle access to the saltpans, but there seem to be no restrictions for pedestrians. It is thus possible to enter on foot and walk along the main tracks that separate the various tanks.

As is usually the case with saltpans, this place is better during high tide, when many waterbirds use it as a roosting site. In autumn and winter there are often large flocks of gulls (including Audouin's and Slender-billed) as well as good numbers of Caspian Terns. Waders are usually plentiful and sometimes form dense mixed flocks – it is worth scrutinizing them carefully, in order to pick out less common species. Flamingos and Spoonbills are also regular at this location.

In spring and summer, the variety of birds is smaller, but apart from the breeding birds, mentioned in the above list, this place also attracts many waders on passage, especially in April and September.

There are more saltpan complexes further north, along the road to Pozo del Camino, however many of them are fenced off.

It may be a good idea to take a look at the estuary of the river Carreras, which lies just south of the saltpans – many birds feed there during low tide. The harbour of Isla Cristina is also worth a stop, as it usually attracts many gulls and is thus a good place for reading colour rings.

15

El Prado lagoon

A small freshwater wetland with large patches of emergent vegetation.

Birds

Resident: Shelduck, Gadwall, Pochard, Red-crested Pochard, Little Grebe, Cattle Egret, White Stork, Marsh Harrier, Kestrel, Coot, Purple Swamphen, Black-winged Stilt, Avocet, Hoopoe, Iberian Green Woodpecker, Crested Lark, Cetti's Warbler, Southern Grey Shrike, Iberian Magpie, Raven, Spotless Starling, Serin, Waxbill

Breeding visitors: Black Kite, Collared Pratincole, Little Ringed Plover, Swift, Pallid Swift, Bee-eater, Sand Martin, Red-rumped Swallow, Savi's Warbler, Reed Warbler, Great Reed Warbler

Non-breeding visitors: Teal, Shoveler, Glossy Ibis, Spoonbill, Flamingo, Buzzard, Booted Eagle, Lapwing, Golden Plover, Ruff, Snipe, Green Sandpiper, Crag Martin, Water Pipit, Penduline Tit

How to visit it

This place lies very close to the village of La Redondela. To get here, leave the A-49 on exit nr. 122 following signs to Isla Cristina. At Pozo del Camino, take the road HU-3300 to La Redondela, which lies 4 km away. At this village, proceed to the northern side and look for a small car workshop called 'Reducto Motor' (37.2235, -7.2711).

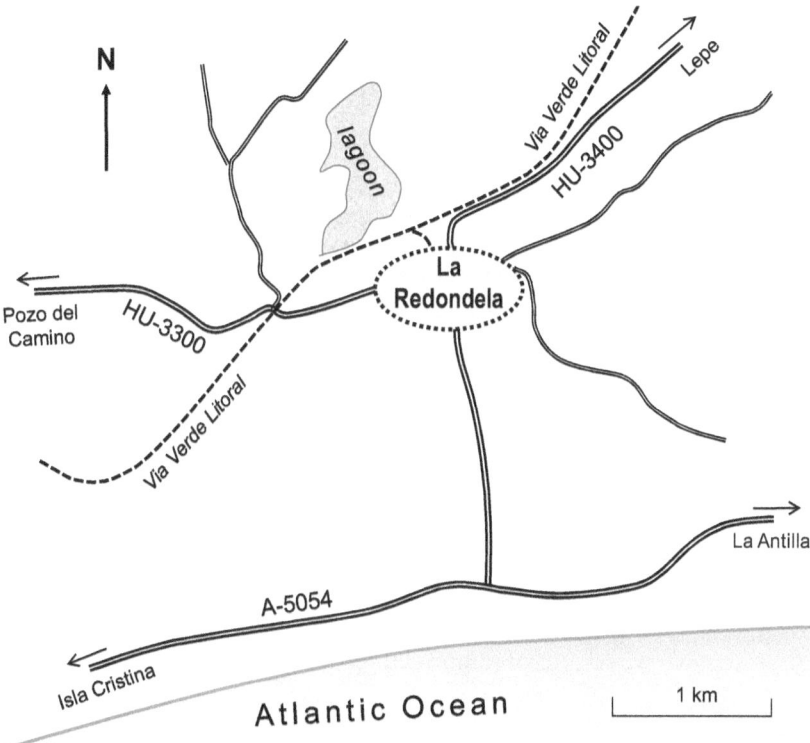

The lagoon must be approached on foot, but the trail is entirely flat, so it is quite easy. From the car workshop, there is a trail going northwards. At first, it goes amid some canes and orchards. About 100 metres ahead, a small tennis court appears on the left. Just after passing this court, one reaches the main trail. This trail, which runs along the former railway line, is part of the 'Via Verde Litoral', a pedestrian route connecting Huelva to Ayamonte. Follow the main trail to the left, until a red building appears on the left side – this is the old railway station. The lagoon starts to appear on the opposite side.

The reedbeds are extensive, and although there is no access to the water, much can be seen from the trail. On the right-hand side, there are two small wooden platforms overlooking the area, which are ideal places to stop and scan. Waterfowl, Purple Swamphen, waders, flamingos, egrets and Marsh Harrier are often around.

Water level can vary a lot throughout the year. In late summer, the place is often dry, and when that is the case most waterbirds are absent.

Cartaya pinewood

An extensive woodland of mature Umbrella Pine.

Birds

Resident: Wood Pigeon, Hoopoe, Iberian Green Woodpecker, Great Spotted Woodpecker, Woodlark, Stonechat, Mistle Thrush, Dartford Warbler, Sardinian Warbler, Long-tailed Tit, Crested Tit, Short-toed Treecreeper, Nuthatch, Jay, Iberian Magpie, Raven, Spotless Starling, Tree Sparrow, Chaffinch, Serin, Cirl Bunting, Corn Bunting

Breeding visitors: Booted Eagle, Cuckoo, Pallid Swift, Red-rumped Swallow, Nightingale, Black-eared Wheatear, Iberian Chiffchaff, Woodchat Shrike

Non-breeding visitors: Robin, Chiffchaff

How to visit it

This pinewood lies about 20 km northwest of Huelva. The easiest way to get there is to take the motorway A-49 and leave it on exit nr.105 following signs to Tariquejo (road HU-3402). After about 1.5 km veer left where signposted 'Presa del piedras'. The pinewood begins here.

This forest is an excellent spot to find several woodland birds that are very scarce in coastal areas and are much easier to see here.

The whole area is quite uniform, and exploration can be done anywhere. Many tracks cross the forest, and they can be used freely to roam. Some reference points are provided below.

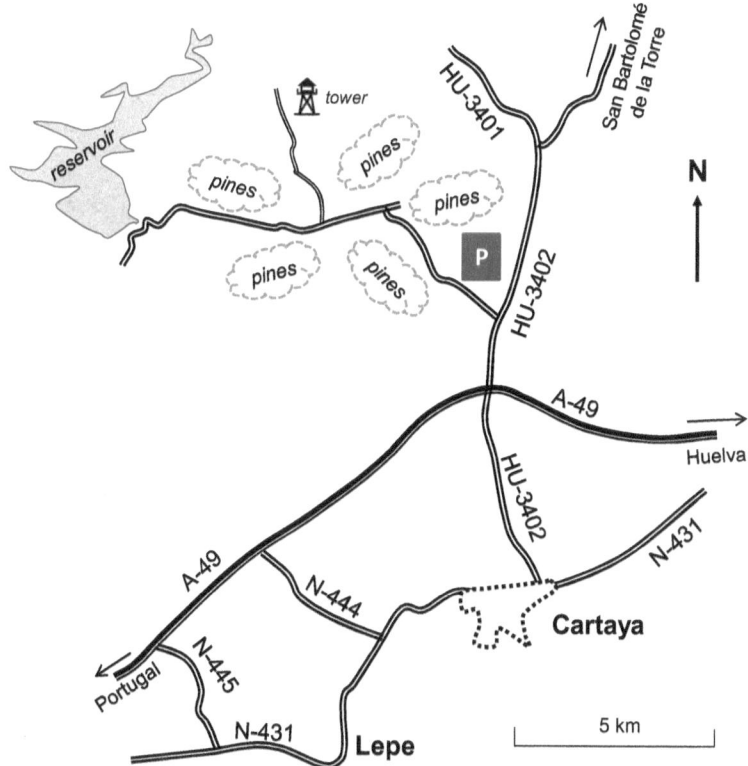

Shortly after entering the pinewood, a resting area appears on the right side (37.3523, -7.1584). It is called 'Las Palomas'. This is an excellent spot to park and explore. Typical birds at this place include various tits and Short-toed Treecreeper. This resting site can be crowded on weekends but is usually quiet during weekdays.

The road continues through the forest, and it pays off to explore other spots along the way. The best approach is to look for side tracks, where it is possible to park safely and walk around. After about 3.5 km there is a T-junction, where one should veer left. 1.5 km ahead, there is a dirt road going right signposted 'Villanueva de los Castillejos'. This road is fairly quiet and is also a good option. It leads to a fire lookout tower. Species that have been recorded along this road include Dartford Warbler, Cirl Bunting and Black-eared Wheatear.

19

River Piedras marshes

An L-shaped estuary with saltmarsh, mudflats and some pinewoods.

Birds

Resident: Cattle Egret, Little Egret, Marsh Harrier, Kentish Plover, Hoopoe, Iberian Green Woodpecker, Crested Lark, Cetti's Warbler, Zitting Cisticola, Long-tailed Tit, Crested Tit, Southern Grey Shrike, Iberian Magpie, Raven, Serin, Linnet, Common Waxbill

Breeding visitors: Montagu's Harrier, Little Tern, Great Spotted Cuckoo, Pallid Swift, Red-rumped Swallow, Iberian Yellow Wagtail

Non-breeding visitors: Gannet, Great Cormorant, Great White Egret, Spoonbill, Osprey, Oystercatcher, Avocet, Grey Plover, Ringed Plover, Knot, Dunlin, Bar-tailed Godwit, Whimbrel, Curlew, Redshank, Greenshank, Turnstone, Mediterranean Gull, Caspian Tern, Sandwich Tern, Kingfisher, Meadow Pipit, Bluethroat, Dartford Warbler

How to visit it

Access is via the N-431 which runs through Cartaya and Lepe. There are two main routes to visit this area.

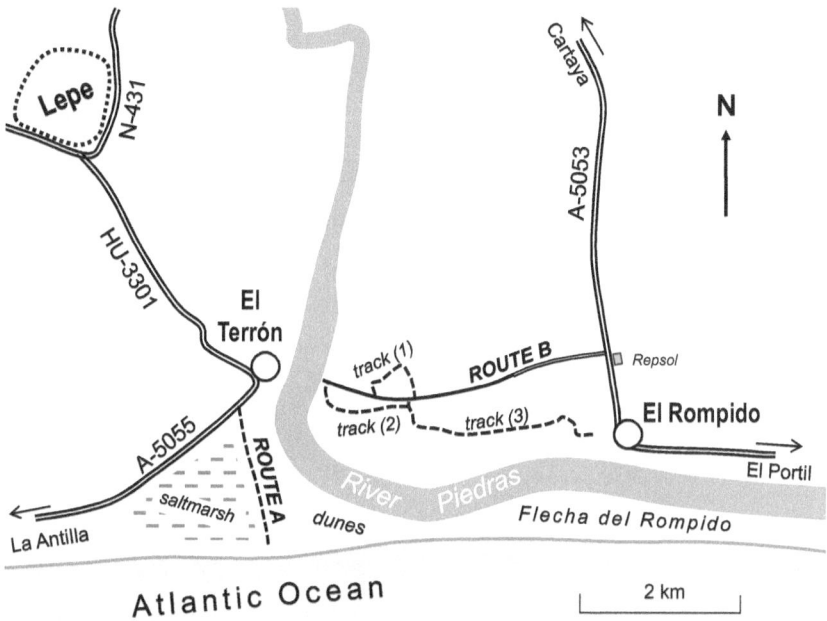

Route A (western bank): leave Lepe southwards on the HU-3301 and proceed to El Terrón. At this location, there is a small harbour which is a convenient place to stop and take a look at the estuary. During low tide, there are usually waders, gulls and other waterbirds. After that, leave El Terrón southwards on the road to La Antilla; 100 m ahead veer left on an unpaved road (starts at 37.2234, -7.1774). This road, which is in poor condition, crosses a vast area of saltmarsh with some channels, which attract waders and egrets. It ends at a small car park close to the beach. To the east, there is a long sandspit ('Flecha del Rompido'). This sandspit is perhaps too long to do on foot, but it is worth walking 1 or 2 km along the shore of the estuary, in order to look for more waterbirds.

Route B (eastern bank): this route lies west of the road linking Cartaya to El Rompido (A-5053). About 7 km south of Cartaya, just before the Repsol petrol station, there is a road to the right (37.2280, -7.1268), which leads to the wetland. This road is tarmac at first, but after a while it becomes unpaved. There are three marked trails, all worth visiting. Track 1 ('Marismas de San Miguel') lies on the right-hand side, it is a circular trail that goes through an area of saltmarsh, which in winter has various waders, egrets and Bluethroat. Track 2 ('La Turbera') runs parallel to the dirt road, through a small forest of Umbrella Pines, which holds several forest birds, including Crested Tit, and leads to the river shore. Track 3 ('Rio Piedras') is much longer, starts at the same place but leads eastwards to El Rompido.

El Portil lagoon

A coastal lagoon surrounded by pines.

Birds

Resident: Mallard, Gadwall, Pochard, Red-crested Pochard, Little Grebe, Great Crested Grebe, Little Egret, Coot, Black-winged Stilt, Yellow-legged Gull, Hoopoe, Iberian Green Woodpecker, Cetti's Warbler, Dartford Warbler, Sardinian Warbler, Long-tailed Tit, Crested Tit, Short-toed Treecreeper, Spotless Starling, Tree Sparrow, Waxbill

Breeding visitors: Turtle Dove, Swift, Pallid Swift, Red-rumped Swallow, Spotted Flycatcher

Non-breeding visitors: Teal, Pintail, Shoveler, Ferruginous Duck, Tufted Duck, White-headed Duck, Black-necked Grebe, Cormorant, Great White Egret, Grey Heron, Glossy Ibis, Green Sandpiper, Audouin's Gull, Kingfisher, Song Thrush, Chiffchaff

How to visit it

This lagoon is located at El Portil, about 10 km southwest of Huelva. Access from the last-named town is made following the A-497 to Punta

Umbria, leaving it at exit no. 9 and following the signs to El Portil. When arriving at this town, take the rightmost lane and park 200 m ahead, where this lane gets wider. A small wooden platform on the roadside (37.2114, -7.0451) offers a good view over the lagoon. This place is very accessible, and its watching platform is particularly suitable for people with disabilities. The platform faces north; therefore, the light conditions are usually good.

It is worth staying here for a while, scanning along the edge of the water, as the birds come in and out of the vegetation. The lagoon usually holds a fine selection of waterbirds, especially ducks and grebes. The rare White-headed Duck has been recorded on several occasions. The only drawback of this platform is the fact that it lies very close to the main road, so the noise from the traffic may be annoying.

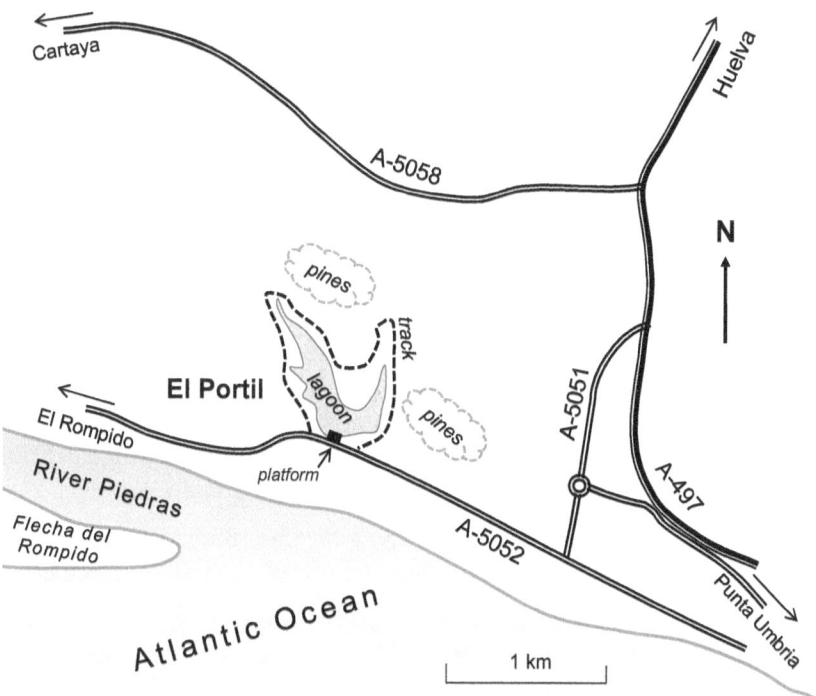

It is, however, possible to walk around the lagoon, thus avoiding the noise. A marked circular trail ('sendero') that goes along the fence is probably the best option. This path goes mostly through pinewood, which is home to several forest birds, including woodpeckers, tits and Short-toed Treecreeper. Furthermore, it is possible to look at the lagoon from different angles and inspect some parts that are not visible from the platform. The circuit is about 3.5 km long.

Odiel marshes and estuary

A large estuary with saltpans, saltmarsh, and dunes.

Birds

Resident: Shelduck, Gadwall, Red-crested Pochard, Little Egret, Spoonbill, Flamingo, Marsh Harrier, Osprey, Black-winged Stilt, Avocet, Kentish Plover, Hoopoe, Crested Lark, Sardinian Warbler

Breeding visitors: Black Kite, Montagu's Harrier, Booted Eagle, Turtle Dove, Little Tern, Pallid Swift, Iberian Yellow Wagtail, Reed Warbler

Non-breeding visitors: Shoveler, Red-breasted Merganser, Black-necked Grebe, Cormorant, Great White Egret, Oystercatcher, Little Stint, Sanderling, Black-tailed Godwit, Bar-tailed Godwit, Whimbrel, Curlew, Redshank, Greenshank, Turnstone, Slender-billed Gull, Audouin's Gull, Caspian Tern, Sandwich Tern, Kingfisher, Skylark, Meadow Pipit, Water Pipit, Bluethroat, Penduline Tit, Spanish Sparrow

How to visit it

There is one main road leading into the reserve. It starts at a roundabout near Corrales (exit nr. 3 from motorway A-497).

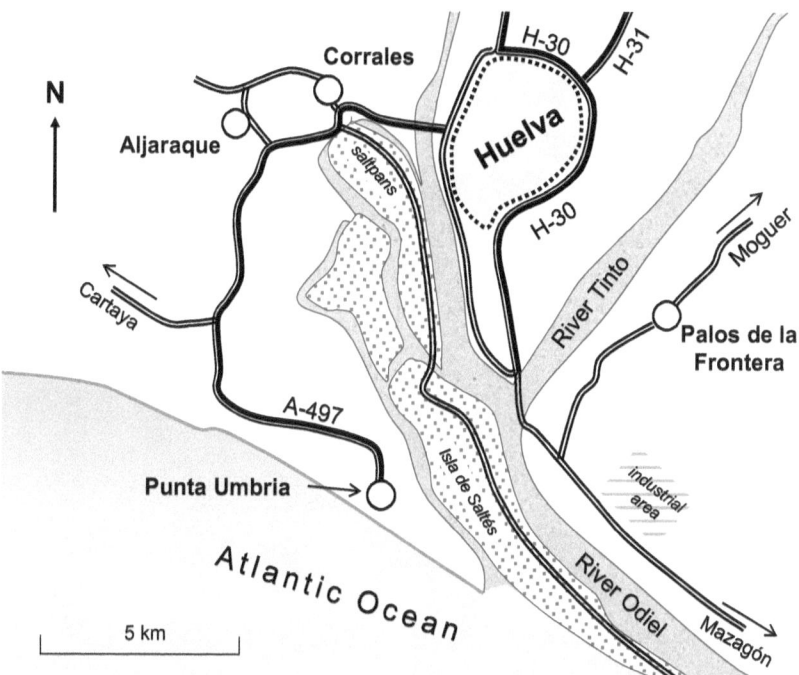

Along the first few km, there is an extensive area of industrial salt works, which attract many waders and flamingos. After about 2.5 km there is a small road to the left signposted 'CREA-CEGMA'. Just next to the gate, there is a pond on the left-hand side (37.2542, -6.9695). This is an excellent location for waterfowl, especially in winter. Purple Swamphen is regular here, and in late summer there are often waders. A small hide has been built on the western side, next to the main road.

Back on the main road, and 250 m further south, there is a gate on the left. This is the entrance to the information centre (open Mon-Sat, 9 am-3 pm). Here one can ask for information about the park and the existing trails. Two trails actually start here: one to the traditional saltpans (1) and another one to 'Calatilla Bacuta' (2). Both of them have a good variety of waterbirds, including waders, gulls, herons and flamingos. Behind the centre, it is also possible to take a look at river Odiel, where there are often grebes, mergansers and cormorants and more waders.

The road continues southwards, passes a tall bridge (Puente del Burro) and enters an island (Isla de Saltés). This island is mostly saltmarsh. There are a few pine plantations along the way, which are worth a look, as they attract passerines, especially on migration. After a while, there is an area of dunes and the road ends at the Espigón Juan Carlos I. There are some car parks on the right-hand side, and from here it is just a short walk to the beach, where one can look at the sea.

Estero de Domingo Rubio

A series of freshwater marshes, bordered by emergent vegetation and surrounded by Umbrella Pine forests.

Birds

Resident: Mallard, Gadwall, Little Grebe, Great Crested Grebe, Little Egret, Spoonbill, Glossy Ibis, White Stork, Marsh Harrier, Water Rail, Moorhen, Coot, Purple Swamphen, Black-winged Stilt, Hoopoe, Cetti's Warbler, Zitting Cisticola, Sardinian Warbler, Long-tailed Tit, Penduline Tit, Iberian Magpie, Raven, Serin, Waxbill

Breeding visitors: Little Bittern, Night Heron, Purple Heron, Bee-eater, Wryneck, Red-rumped Swallow, Iberian Yellow Wagtail, Nightingale, Reed Warbler, Great Reed Warbler, Iberian Chiffchaff

Non-breeding visitors: Cormorant, Great White Egret, Osprey, Ruff, Green Sandpiper, Kingfisher, Bluethroat, Song Thrush, Sedge Warbler

How to visit it

This wetland lies a few km southeast of Huelva, not far from the place where river Tinto meets river Odiel. It is best accessed through the

A-494 linking Moguer to Mazagón. About 4 km south of the former town, shortly after km 16 mark, look for a narrow road to the right (37.2060, -6.8726). This road leads along the northern edge of a wetland. There are many patches of reeds and reedmace and also some trees, mainly willows. After about 1 km there is a wooden platform, which can also be used to inspect the area.

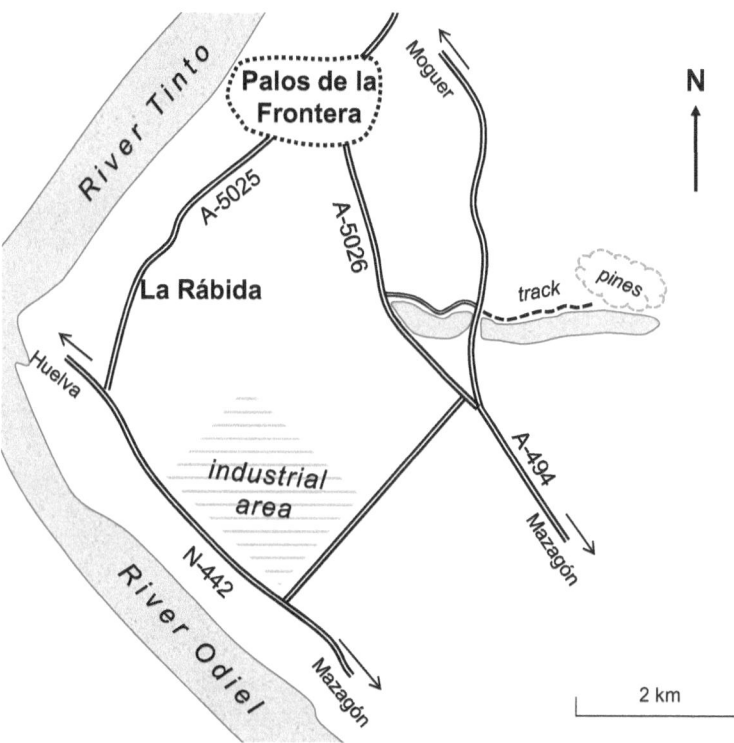

Back to the main road, on the opposite side there is a sandy track leading eastwards. This track, which is probably best done on foot, also goes along the wetland. On this side, there are vast expanses of emergent vegetation, where Reed and Great Reed Warblers are plentiful in spring. Other waterbirds typically include herons, Cormorant, Purple Swamphen, grebes and sometimes a few ducks. The wetland is bordered by trees, and it is worth scrutinizing them carefully, as they attract a variety of passerines, including tits and warblers. Cetti's Warbler is abundant, Penduline Tit breeds, Sedge Warbler occurs on passage, while Nightingale and Iberian Chiffchaff are summer visitors.

After a while, the track enters a pinewood. Birds recorded here include Wryneck, Short-toed Treecreeper and Long-tailed Tit.

Palos lagoon

A small freshwater lagoon surrounded by emergent vegetation.

Birds

Resident: Mallard, Gadwall, Pochard, Red-crested Pochard, Little Grebe, Little Egret, Glossy Ibis, Marsh Harrier, Moorhen, Coot, Purple Swamphen, Cetti's Warbler, Long-tailed Tit, Penduline Tit, Iberian Magpie, Spotless Starling, Serin, Waxbill

Breeding visitors: Night Heron, Squacco Heron, Purple Heron, Whiskered Tern, Bee-eater, Nightingale

Non-breeding visitors: Teal, Pintail, Shoveler, Cormorant, Osprey, Kingfisher

How to visit it

The Palos lagoon (locally known as 'Laguna Primera de Palos') is the westernmost and the second largest of a lagoon complex called 'Paraje Natural de las Lagunas de Palos y de las Madres'. It lies next to the Huelva industrial area. Access to this location is easy: leave Huelva southwards on the N-442 following signs to Mazagón. The road crosses the river Tinto and then runs through a large industrial area for about 4 km. When the industrial area ends, look for a track on the left side (37.1700, -6.8944) and park. The lagoon lies just nearby.

An old railway line runs parallel to the road, and from here it is possible to see a large portion of the wetland. It is worth staying here for a while, scanning the water and the surrounding vegetation. Ducks and grebes are frequently seen on the water. Along the edges, there are often herons, ibises and Purple Swamphen, but these birds tend to feed among the vegetation, so it usually pays off to scan the shore carefully.

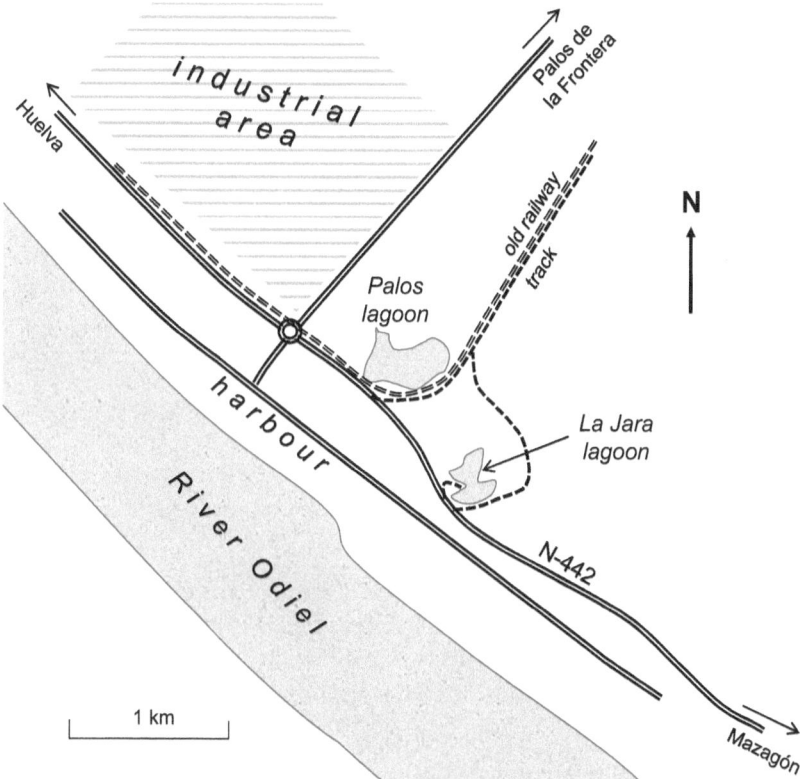

A hide is visible in the middle of the lagoon. This hide is managed by an oil company; unfortunately, it is usually closed to visitors.

The other sides of the lagoon are less easy to get to, as there are no tracks or marked trails.

About 800m to the southeast, along the N-442, there is another lagoon (Laguna de la Jara) with a small bird hide. Although it lies very close to the road, access can be a bit tricky, as there is no place to park safely. Two small tracks lead to the edge of the lagoon.

Doñana – El Rocío

A typical Andalusian village, noted for its annual pilgrimage. Just in front of it lies a large flooded area which definitely deserves a stop.

Birds

Resident: Greylag Goose, Gadwall, Pochard, Red-crested Pochard, Little Grebe, Little Egret, Glossy Ibis, Spoonbill, White Stork, Flamingo, Marsh Harrier, Purple Swamphen, Coot, Black-winged Stilt, Hoopoe, Crested Lark, Cetti's Warbler, Spotless Starling, Waxbill

Breeding visitors: Little Bittern, Squacco Heron, Night Heron, Purple Heron, Black Kite, Collared Pratincole, Whiskered Tern, Turtle Dove, Swift, Pallid Swift, Sand Martin, Red-rumped Swallow, Yellow Wagtail, Reed Warbler, Great Reed Warbler

Non-breeding visitors: Teal, Pintail, Shoveler, Sparrowhawk, Lapwing, Black-tailed Godwit, Snipe, Greenshank, Bluethroat, Penduline Tit

How to visit it

Probably the main gateway to Doñana National Park, El Rocío is a popular town. It is very accessible and an excellent starting point for those who visit Doñana for the first time. The easiest way to get there is to follow the A-483 which connects the A-49 highway to Matalascañas. The main attraction here is the Marisma del Rocío, a flooded area that lies immediately south of the village. This location attracts many waterbirds, and large flocks can be seen here throughout the year. During winter there are usually many ducks, along with flamingos, spoonbills and various waders. In spring there are often terns, Collared Pratincoles and many Black Kites.

A broad avenue called 'Mirador de la Marisma' (37.1316, -6.4878) runs along the southern edge of the village and is the most convenient way to explore this area. Parking is available here. The avenue offers an excellent view over most of the wetland. Its only drawback is its orientation: it faces south, meaning that you will be looking against sunlight for much of the day. At its eastern end, there are patches of reeds, which are favoured by Little Bittern, Reed and Great Reed Warblers in spring and by Bluethroat and Penduline Tit in winter.

Just east of these reed beds, lies the ornithological centre 'Francisco Bernis' (open Wednesday to Sunday, 10 am – 2 pm). From the top terrace, it is possible to enjoy superb views over the marisma.

The western shore of the marisma can also be explored along the track that runs parallel to the main N-483. A few hides have been built here. Watching from this side is better during the afternoon.

Doñana – La Rocina

A lake with large patches of emergent vegetation.

Birds

Resident: Gadwall, Pochard, Red-crested Pochard, Little Grebe, Little Egret, Glossy Ibis, Spoonbill, Marsh Harrier, Purple Swamphen, Kingfisher, Hoopoe, Woodlark, Cetti's Warbler, Dartford Warbler, Long-tailed Tit, Crested Tit, Short-toed Treecreeper, Penduline Tit, Iberian Magpie, Raven, Spotless Starling, Serin, Hawfinch, Waxbill

Breeding visitors: Little Bittern, Night Heron, Purple Heron, Black Kite, Booted Eagle, Cuckoo, Bee-eater, Sand Martin, Nightingale, Savi's Warbler, Reed Warbler, Great Reed Warbler, Melodious Warbler, Iberian Chiffchaff, Spotted Flycatcher, Woodchat Shrike

Non-breeding visitors: Teal, Shoveler, Black Redstart, Redwing, Firecrest

How to visit it

Lying immediately west of El Rocío (see p. 30), the information centre of La Rocina is quite easy to find: leave El Rocío southwards, on the

A-483 road to Matalascañas. Just after passing the bridge, turn right – the information centre is right there (37.1236, -6.4965). The gate leading to this area is open from 8 am to 10 pm. Free parking is available.

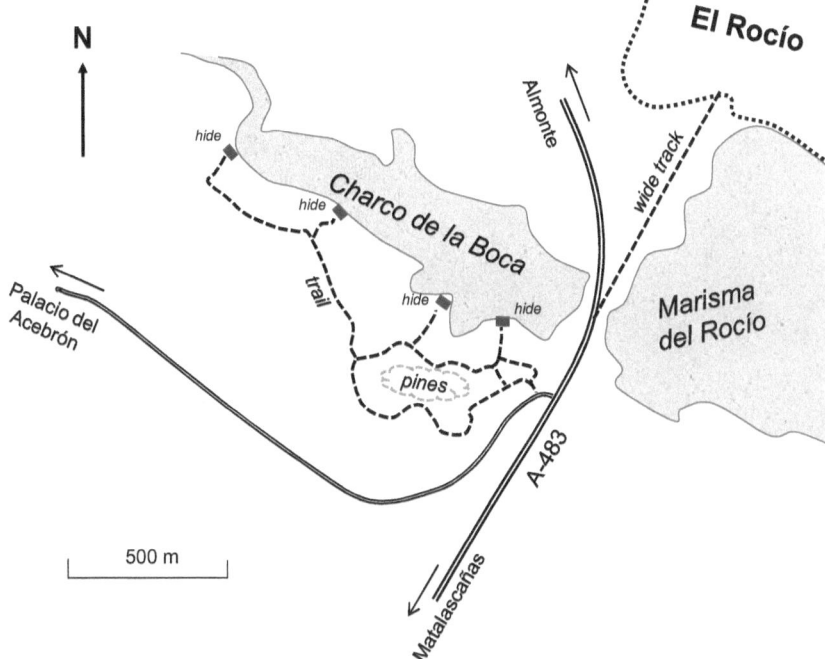

Visits are made on foot, using the existing trails (which are in fact boardwalks). These trails lead to a set of four hides overlooking the wetland. All hides face north, so light is usually perfect for birdwatching and photography. There are many patches of emergent vegetation, which attract a lot of interesting birds.

During springtime, it is usually possible to find an array of herons and warblers, along with waterfowl, Spoonbill, Glossy Ibis and Purple Swamphen. The reedbeds are alive with the songs of breeding Cetti's, Savi's and Reed Warblers. Typical birds at the lake include waterfowl, egrets, ibises and spoonbills. In autumn and winter, the place is usually quieter, as most birds tend to gather at the nearby Marisma del Rocío (see p. 30). It should be noted that the lake may dry up during summer.

The boardwalks cross some fine areas of pinewood. These woods hold several forest birds, including Crested Tit, Short-toed Treecreeper and Serin. There are also some tracts of riparian forest, which form the ideal habitat of Nightingale, Melodious Warbler and Iberian Chiffchaff. The trail leading to the two westernmost hides crosses an area of scrub, which has Woodlark and Dartford Warbler.

Doñana – Palacio del Acebrón

Riverine forest and pinewood.

Birds

Resident: Night Heron, Kingfisher, Lesser Spotted Woodpecker, Wren, Cetti's Warbler, Dartford Warbler, Sardinian Warbler, Blackcap, Firecrest, Long-tailed Tit, Crested Tit, Short-toed Treecreeper, Iberian Magpie, Spotless Starling, Serin, Cirl Bunting, Waxbill

Breeding visitors: Cuckoo, Nightingale, Reed Warbler, Melodious Warbler, Iberian Chiffchaff, Spotted Flycatcher, Woodchat Shrike

Non-breeding visitors: Robin, Chiffchaff

How to visit it

Access is made through the gate leading to La Rocina centre (see p. 32), but instead of parking there, just proceed for another 3 km until the road ends at a car park (37.1420, -6.5457). A circular trail starts here. It is about 1.5 km long. The following description applies when the trail is walked in the counterclockwise direction (but it can also be walked in the opposite way).

At first, the trail goes among some oaks and pines, with riverine forest on the left side. Typical birds in spring include Nightingale, Cetti's Warbler and Iberian Chiffchaff. After a while, there are some boardwalks that cross the stream, amid riverine forest and patches of reeds. The vegetation is very dense, and birds are more often heard than seen. In spring it is easy to hear the songs of Nightingale, Reed and Melodious Warblers.

On the other side of the river, there are some areas of mature pine. This habitat is favoured by birds of dry woodland, such as Lesser Spotted Woodpecker, Spotted Flycatcher, Crested Tit, Short-toed Treecreeper, and Iberian Magpie.

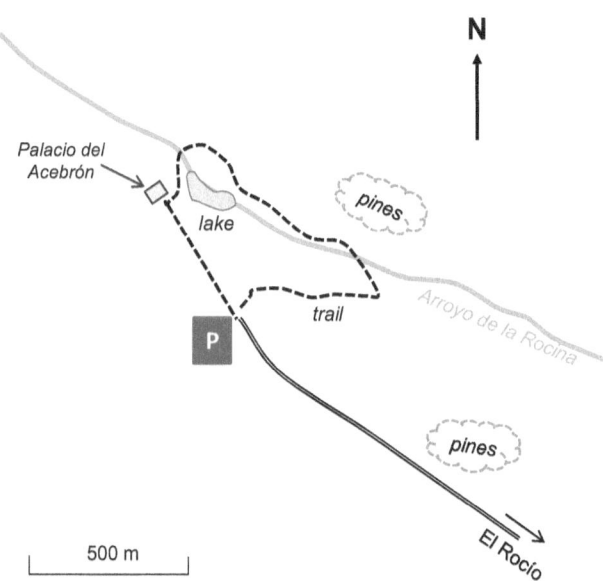

Finally, another boardwalk appears – the trail crosses the stream again and enters an open area. A large white building can be seen – this is the Palacio del Acebrón. It is open to visitors (information panels inside).

There are also two wooden platforms, from where it is possible to take a look at a small lake ('Charco del Acebrón'). Night Herons are sometimes seen here, roosting in the trees.

This location can be visited at any time of year, but spring is probably the best time to find a greater diversity of species, as many songbirds are singing actively and can be easily located by their sounds. In winter most birds are silent and therefore difficult to find in the dense forest.

Doñana – El Acebuche

A set of lagoons equipped with observatories.

Birds

Resident: Mallard, Pochard, Red-Crested Pochard, Little Grebe, White Stork, Purple Swamphen, Wood Pigeon, Stonechat, Dartford Warbler, Sardinian Warbler, Crested Tit, Short-toed Treecreeper, Southern Grey Shrike, Iberian Magpie, Spotless Starling, Tree Sparrow, Corn Bunting

Breeding visitors: Purple Heron, Black Kite, Booted Eagle, Bee-eater, Melodious Warbler, Woodchat Shrike, Golden Oriole

Non-breeding visitors: Snipe, Green Sandpiper, Robin, Black Redstart

How to visit it

Access is via the N-483 which connects El Rocío to Matalascañas. About 3 km north of the last-named place, there is a road signposted 'El Acebuche', which leads to the information centre (37.0463, -6.5662). Free parking is available.

This location can only be visited on foot. A set of marked paths make exploration easy. There are two main trails: the Acebuche Lagoon Path and the Path of the Huerto and Las Pajas Lagoons. These trails go through the pinewoods which hold many Iberian Magpies and other forest birds.

The first path leads to the largest lagoon (Laguna del Acebuche). Six birdwatching hides have been built along its southern side. All hides face north and offer a view over the lagoon.

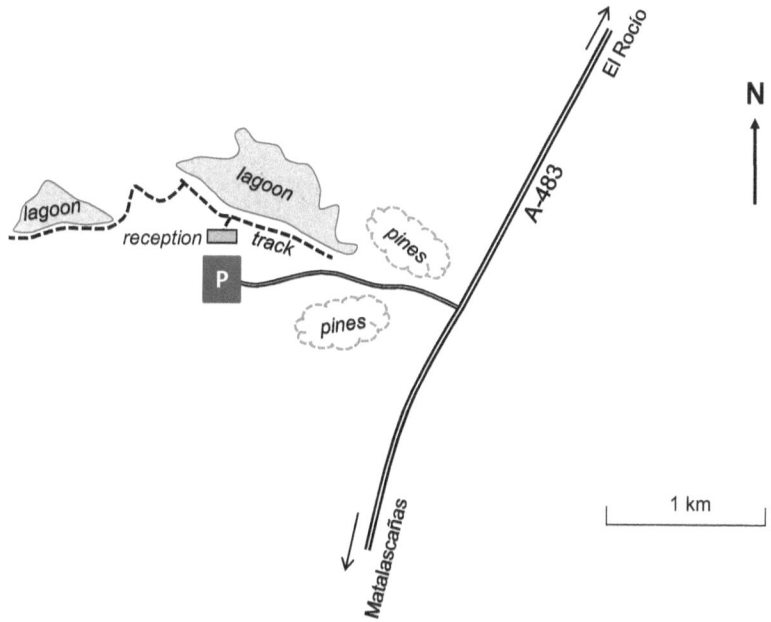

The other path is a bit longer and leads westwards towards Laguna de las Pajas and Laguna del Huerto (the latter is not plotted on the above map). Each of these lagoons has its own bird hide as well. A map of the trails can be obtained at the visitors centre.

For many years, El Acebuche has been one of the key places to visit in Doñana. This centre is equipped with good infrastructures (trails and hides), as well as an audiovisual show about the National Park. It is also the place where visits to the more restricted areas of the National Park can be booked. It should, however, be noted that the lagoons of El Acebuche are nowadays much less interesting for birdwatching than they used to be. Indeed, in the past, this location used to attract a good number of waterbirds, but in recent years the number of birds seems to be much lower. The reasons for this are not very clear. It is possible that birds now prefer other sites within the National Park. Additionally, as is the case with La Rocina (see p. 32), the lagoons may dry up during summer and when that is the case there are no waterbirds around.

Campiña de Huelva

An area of non-irrigated cereal crops and olive groves.

Birds

Resident: Quail, Cattle Egret, Black-shouldered Kite, Griffon Vulture, Marsh Harrier, Buzzard, Kestrel, Little Owl, Hoopoe, Calandra Lark, Crested Lark, Crag Martin, Stonechat, Cetti's Warbler, Zitting Cisticola, Southern Grey Shrike, Raven, Spanish Sparrow, Serin, Corn Bunting

Breeding visitors: Black Kite, Montagu's Harrier, Short-toed Eagle, Booted Eagle, Lesser Kestrel, Turtle Dove, Swift, Bee-eater, Short-toed Lark, Red-rumped Swallow, Iberian Yellow Wagtail, Nightingale, Black-eared Wheatear, Reed Warbler, Great Reed Warbler, Olivaceous Warbler, Melodious Warbler, Golden Oriole, Woodchat Shrike

Non-breeding visitors: Red Kite, Hen Harrier, Skylark, Meadow Pipit

How to visit it

This area lies northeast of Huelva and forms a long strip of fields about 60 km long and 7 km wide. It consists mostly of treeless fields, but in some sectors, there are olive groves as well.

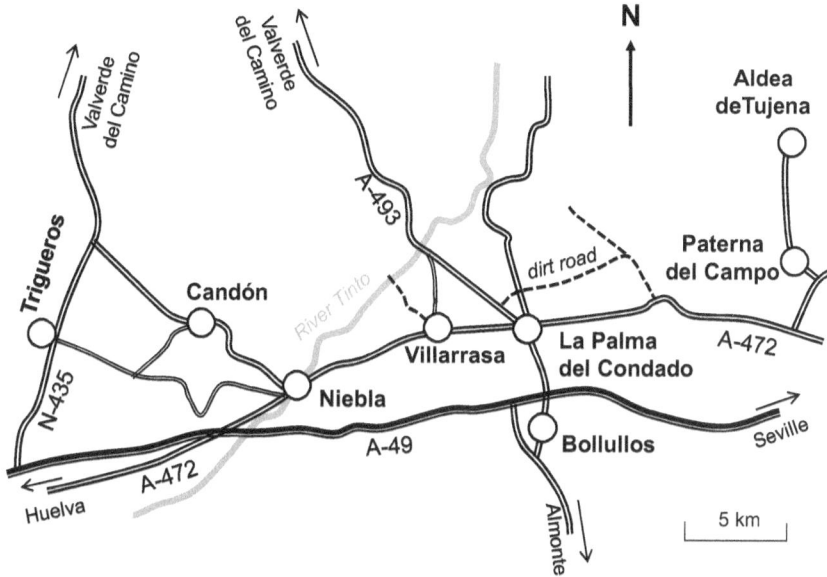

Several roads cross the area. The best strategy is to follow secondary roads, which are usually quiet, and making regular stops, especially near hilltops, in order to scan. There are also many dirt roads and tracks crossing the fields. Some routes are suggested here.

In the westernmost sector, there is an accessible area between Trigueros and Candón. Leave Trigueros eastwards (a look at the large water deposit may produce breeding Lesser Kestrels) and proceed eastwards through the fields. Calandra Larks are frequent along this route. After about 5 km, veer left and take the road towards Candón.

At Niebla, the bridge over river Tinto (37.3649, -6.6741) is a good place to watch Crag Martins.

Further east, another interesting sector lies around Palma del Condado and Villarrasa. Soaring vultures sometimes appear over this sector, and Red Kite is frequent in winter. This area has many nests of White Storks on the electricity pylons. From Villarrasa, it is worth exploring two small roads leading northwards. The leftmost one (unsurfaced) leads to a bridge over river Tinto; the river is bordered by reed beds where Cetti's and Great Reed Warblers occur.

The area north of Paterna del Campo is also easy to explore – try along the road northwards to Aldea de Tujena and then follow one of the dirt roads eastwards to Tejada la Nueva (37.4485, -6.3632). Olivaceous Warbler has been recorded along the stream at the last-named location.

Puebla de Guzmán

A mixed landscape with some *dehesas*, open areas and a few small river beds. There is also an abandoned mine.

Birds

Resident: White Stork, Griffon Vulture, Cinereous Vulture, Goshawk, Eagle Owl, Little Owl, Hoopoe, Iberian Green Woodpecker, Thekla Lark, Woodlark, Crag Martin, Blue Rock Thrush, Dartford Warbler, Sardinian Warbler, Long-tailed Tit, Nuthatch, Southern Grey Shrike, Iberian Magpie, Raven, Spotless Starling, Hawfinch, Corn Bunting

Breeding visitors: Purple Heron, Turtle Dove, Swift, White-rumped Swift, Bee-eater, Red-rumped Swallow, Nightingale, Black-eared Wheatear, Subalpine Warbler, Golden Oriole, Woodchat Shrike

Non-breeding visitors: Red Kite, Lapwing, Green Sandpiper, Skylark

How to visit it

This area lies in western Andévalo, 12 km west of Tharsis (see p. 42). (see p. 42) From Tharsis, continue on the A-475 westwards. If coming from Ayamonte area, follow A-499 through Villanueva de los Castillejos.

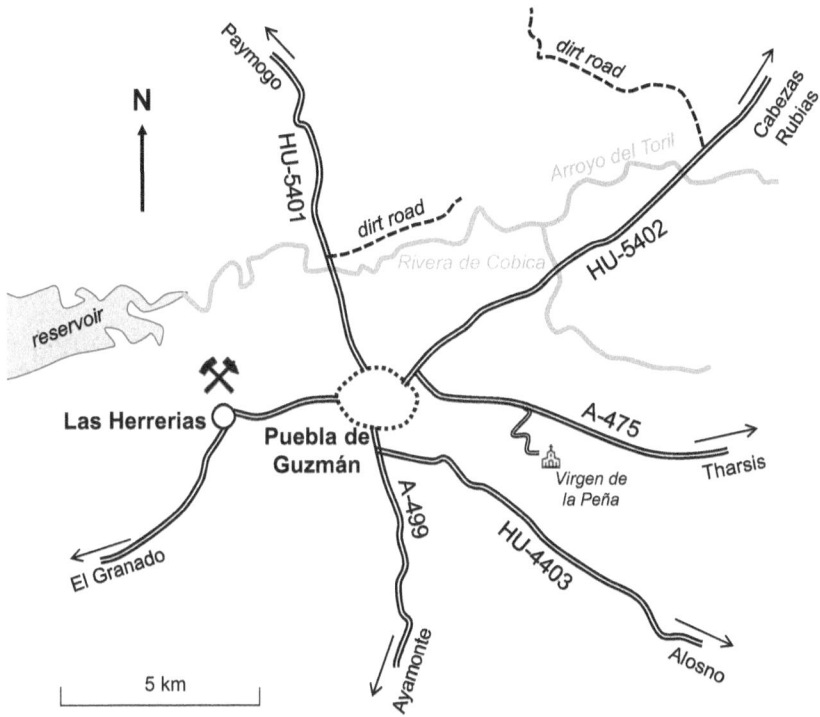

Around Puebla the Guzmán there are several places worth exploring. Some of them are highlighted here.

One of the best roads is the HU-5402 that runs northeastwards towards Cabezas Rubias. This road crosses several small bridges, all worth inspecting. White-rumped Swift has been recorded here, as well as Hawfinch. About 9 km from town, a wide unsurfaced road to the left leads to an area of *dehesas* (holm oaks). Thekla Lark and Woodlark are common in this sector.

North of Puebla de Guzman, the road HU-5401 crosses an area of fields which is good for open country species, including wintering Red Kites.

The western sector also merits some attention. At Las Herrerías there is an old mine (37.6148, -7.2931), which can be explored on foot along the existing tracks. There is much debris around, and this forms optimal habitat for Black-eared Wheatear, which is common here. Other birds in this area include Eagle Owl, Blue Rock Thrush, and Hawfinch.

A few km east, along the A-475 to Tharsis, there is a rocky hill with a chapel at the top. This is another location for White-rumped Swift. It is also a good spot to scan the surrounding area for raptors, especially after mid-morning. Large flocks of vultures sometimes fly over.

Tharsis

A complex of abandoned mines.

Birds

Resident: White Stork, Grey Heron, Griffon Vulture, Kestrel, Thekla Lark, Woodlark, Crag Martin, Stonechat, Blue Rock Thrush, Cetti's Warbler, Dartford Warbler, Sardinian Warbler, Southern Grey Shrike, Iberian Magpie, Chough, Raven, Spotless Starling, Rock Sparrow, Linnet, Corn Bunting, Waxbill

Breeding visitors: Purple Heron, Black Stork, Bee-eater, Red-rumped Swallow, Nightingale, Black-eared Wheatear, Subalpine Warbler

Non-breeding visitors: Meadow Pipit, Dunnock, Black Redstart

How to visit it

Tharsis is a small town in central Andévalo region, about 50 km northwest of Huelva. The best way to get there from Huelva is the H-30 to Gibraleón and then the A-495 which links Gibraleón to Tharsis. If coming from the nearby site Puebla de Guzmán (see p. 40), access is via the A-475.

There are two main locations worth visiting: Tharsis mine and Lagunazo mine. The former lies very close to Tharsis town and comprises several large pits just south of the town, east of the A-495. Look for the the GALP petrol station (37.5915, -7.1198). Several roads and tracks start there and lead to the pits. The number of birds at this place is usually small, but Crag Martins are often around (with large flocks in winter), Blue Rock Thrush is regular, Black Stork appears in spring and Griffon Vultures are sometimes seen in the distance. Rock Sparrow has been recorded around the pits, but its status is not very clear.

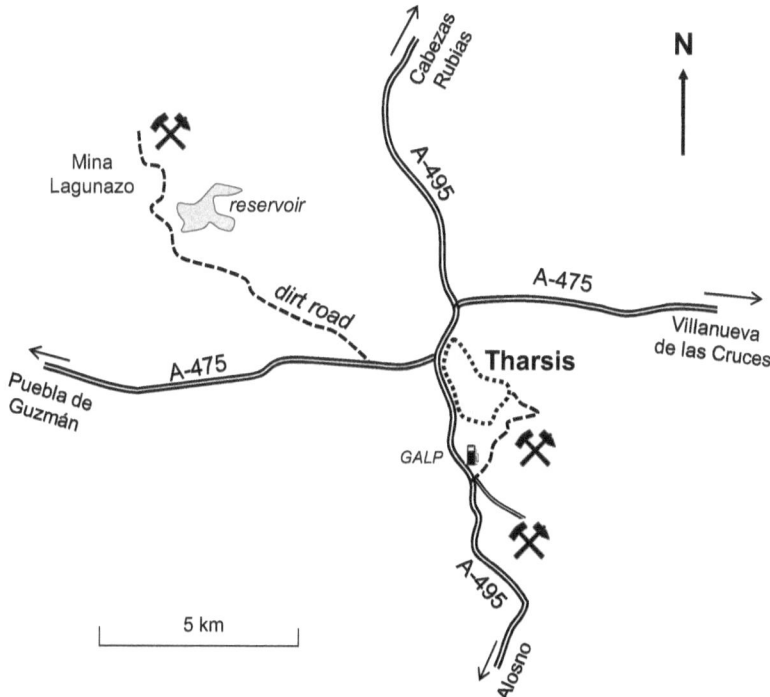

Lagunazo mine is another complex lying about 5 km to the northwest. To get there, look for a dirt road that starts 1 km west of Tharsis, along the road A-475 (37.6044, -7.1363). This dirt road leads to the old mine, which can then be explored on foot. There are several platforms from where it is possible to look at the open pits. This is one of the best places in the entire region to see Eagle Owl, Black Stork and Chough. The owl is, as usual, very elusive, so patience is needed to see it. Try scanning the inaccessible walls, where it often rests during the day. The surrounding hillsides are covered by scrub; typical birds in this habitat include Thekla Lark, Dartford Warbler and wintering Dunnock.

Sierra de Aracena y Picos de Aroche

A mountain area with extensive areas of forest – mostly oak, sweet chestnut, pine and some riverine woodland.

Birds

Resident: Griffon Vulture, Cinereous Vulture, Hoopoe, Great Spotted Woodpecker, Lesser Spotted Woodpecker, Woodlark, Crag Martin, Grey Wagtail, Blue Rock Thrush, Mistle Thrush, Firecrest, Long-tailed Tit, Crested Tit, Nuthatch, Short-toed Treecreeper, Raven, Spotless Starling, Rock Sparrow, Serin, Cirl Bunting

Breeding visitors: Black Kite, Short-toed Eagle, Booted Eagle, Swift, Pallid Swift, Red-rumped Swallow, Nightingale, Redstart, Melodious Warbler, Subalpine Warbler, Iberian Chiffchaff

Non-breeding visitors: Red Kite, Alpine Accentor, Black Redstart, Song Thrush, Bullfinch

How to visit it

This hotspot lies in the far northern part of Huelva province. It belongs to a vast protected area called 'Parque Natural de la Sierra de Aracena y Picos de Aroche'. To get here from Huelva, follow the N-435 northwards for about 100 km until you reach Jabugo.

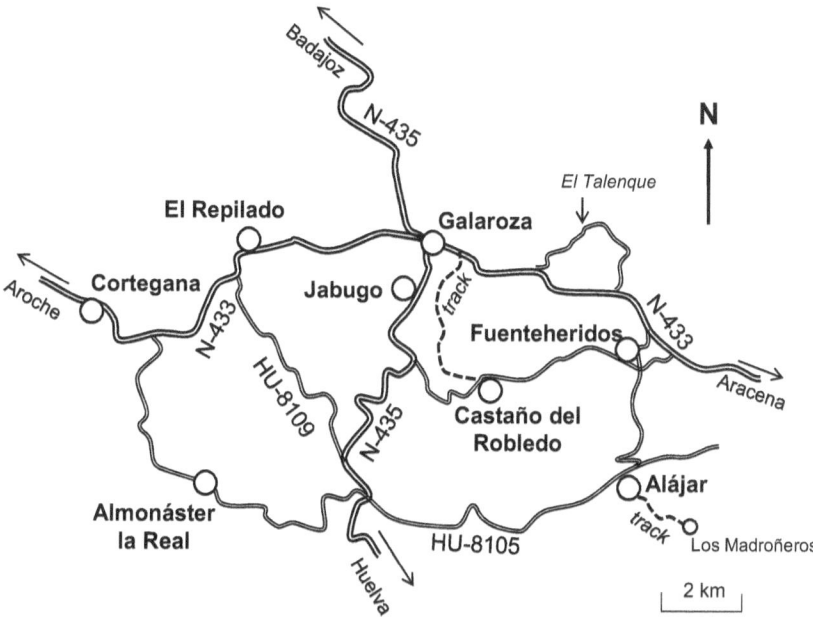

The park is very large, and there are many marked trails ('senderos'), which can be used to explore it. Some locations are suggested here.

- Castaño del Robledo – lies about 5 km southeast of Jabugo. Three marked trails start at this village. One of them, called 'Ribera de Jabugo' (starting point 37.8962, -6.7071) goes northwards along river Jabugo, towards Galaroza. Typical birds along here include Iberian Chiffchaff and Firecrest.

- Alájar – an impressive area with some cliffs and vast expanses of Cork and Holm Oak. A trail starts at the southern tip (37.8726, -6.6627) and goes southeast towards Los Madroñeros. Birds that can be seen along this route include Woodlark and Cirl Bunting. This is also a good location for large birds of prey.

- Area recreativa 'El Talenque' – a recreation area with an interesting patch of Pyrenean Oak (37.9301, -6.6761). Several tracks make it possible to explore the surroundings. Melodious Warbler and Cirl Bunting have been recorded here.

- Cortegana – a small town along the road to Aroche; birds of interest at this location include Alpine Accentor in winter and Blue Rock Thrush year-round – look for them at the castle.

45

About the author

Gonçalo Elias is the author or co-author of twenty books about birds and the best places to watch them, both in English and in Portuguese, including *Guia das Aves de Lisboa, As Aves do Estuário do Tejo, Atlas das Aves Invernantes do Baixo Alentejo, A Birdwatcher's Guide to Portugal, As Aves do Estuário do Sado, Aves de Portugal – Ornitologia do território continental, Birds of Portugal – An Annotated Checklist, Birds of the Algarve and Southern Alentejo,* and *Birding hotspots in the Algarve* (a series of 8 books), along with several papers and notes in specialized ornithological journals.

The author is a founding member of SPEA – Sociedade Portuguesa para o Estudo das Aves (the Portuguese society for the study of birds), and was a member of its board between 1999 and 2002, as well as coordinator of the PRC – the Portuguese Rarities Committee, between 2002 and 2006.

A keen birdwatcher since his teens, Gonçalo Elias has visited over 30 different countries in four continents to watch birds, and has participated in nine bird atlases in Portugal, Spain, and Tanzania.

www.ingramcontent.com/pod-product-compliance
Lightning Source LLC
Chambersburg PA
CBHW031334290526
45784CB00014B/2679